364

SAINT BENEDICT SCHOOL
DUFFIELD ROAD
DERBY DE22 1JD

KV-325-438

T13844

T1384'

T

D30187885
Derbyshire School
Library Service

364

T13844

PAST AND PRESENT

RIOTS

PHILIP STEELE

Smoke billows as a riot breaks out on the Falls Road in Belfast. Northern Ireland has
seen extreme violence on the streets for over 20 years.

© Heinemann Educational Books Ltd, 1993

Apart from any fair dealing for the purposes of research or private study, or criticism or review, as permitted under the Copyright, Designs and Patents Act, 1988, this publication may only be reproduced, stored or transmitted, in any form or by any means, with the prior permission in writing of the publishers, or in the case of reprographic reproduction in accordance with the terms of licences issued by the Copyright Licensing Agency. Enquiries concerning reproduction outside those terms should be sent to the publishers at the undermentioned address.

Any person who does any unauthorised act in relation to this publication may be liable to criminal prosecution and civil claims for damages.

First published in 1993 by Heinemann Library, an imprint of Heinemann Educational, a division of Heinmann Publishers (Oxford) Ltd, Halley Court, Jordan Hill, Oxford OX2 8EJ

OXFORD LONDON EDINBURGH
MADRID PARIS ATHENS BOLOGNA
MELBOURNE SYDNEY AUCKLAND SINGAPORE
TOKYO IBADAN NAIROBI GABORONE HARARE
PORTSMOUTH NH (USA)

Devised and produced by Zoë Books Limited
15 Worthy Lane, Winchester, SO23 7AB, England

Edited by Charlotte Rolfe
Picture research by Faith Perkins
Designed by Julian Holland

Printed in China

A CIP catalogue record for this book is available from the British Library.

ISBN 0 431 06590 X

Photographic acknowledgements

The author and publishers wish to acknowledge, with thanks, the following photographic sources:
Associated Press p21: Hulton-Deutsch Collection pp 6; 10: Magnum pp title page (Chris Steele-Perkins); 39 (Leonard Freed): Popperfoto pp 5; 8; 17; 19; 33: Topham Picture Source pp 15; 16; 23; 25; 27; 30; 37; 41; 42

Cover photograph is courtesy of Magnum/Raghu Rai

The publishers have made every effort to trace the copyright holders, but if they have inadvertently overlooked any, they will be pleased to make the necessary arrangement at the first opportunity.

CONTENTS

ON THE RAMPAGE

Pictures like this one were on the front pages of many newspapers around the world on 1 April 1990. Articles in the newspapers that day described a serious **riot** which had taken place in Britain the day before. What had happened? About 200 000 protesters were demonstrating peacefully against a new form of local taxation, the 'community charge'. However, a few hundred people broke away and rampaged through the West End of London. Shop windows were shattered. Expensive cars were destroyed in their showrooms. Shoppers fled as rioters fought with police. The police fought back furiously in a pitched battle. At the end of the day 450 people were injured. The police made 339 arrests.

The 'community charge' was popularly known as the 'poll tax'. Some of the newspapers pointed out that it was another 'poll tax' that had sparked off a series of riots in the year 1381, during a rising which became known as the Peasants' Revolt. On that occasion the city of London had been set on fire, prisons broken open, and a judge and an archbishop murdered.

Older people sometimes say that rioting never happened in their days. However, riots have taken place in every century – and in every part of the world. In recent years alone, there have been riots in the United States, in the countries of the former Soviet Union, in India and the Far East, in Africa, in Europe.

A man climbs a lamp-post during the London 'poll tax' riot of 1990. Behind him flames rise from a building site set on fire by angry rioters.

Britain's first 'poll tax' riot occurred in 1381, during the Peasants' Revolt. Wat Tyler led poor people from Kent into London. They looted, murdered, released prisoners and burned legal records.

WHAT IS A RIOT?

The term 'riot' is used very broadly. Lawyers have tried to define it more precisely, but their attempts have varied greatly from one country to another, and from one century to another. For example, some have said that a riot must involve at least three people, others twelve.

'Riot' was originally a French word. *Riote* meant a quarrel, a dispute or a debate. It was probably linked to the word *ruir*, 'to make an uproar', and to a word in the Latin language, *rugire* – 'to roar'.

A riot is an undisciplined outbreak of violence. It may be directed against the rulers of a country, the government, the army or police. It may be directed against the public at large, with passers-by being attacked at random. It may also be directed at particular sections of the community, such as factory owners, shopkeepers, followers of a particular religion, foreigners, or **ethnic minorities.**

Rioting normally occurs on the spur of the moment. Tempers fray and suddenly they snap. People lose control. In such situations even the smallest incident, such as an insult or a routine arrest, may act as a flashpoint. The result may take everybody by surprise, both the rioters themselves and the forces of law and order.

Clashes between protesters and the forces of law and order are often far from straightforward, and it may be difficult to find out how the trouble started or who was behind it. For political reasons, some governments may unfairly accuse peaceful, legal demonstrators of being rioters. The police or army may themselves run riot, turning to illegal violence and rampaging through the streets.

'When hopes and dreams are loose in the streets it is well for the timid to lock their doors and lie low until the wrath has passed.'

Eric Hoffer, American philosopher, in
'The True Believer', 1951

ACTS OF VIOLENCE

Riotous behaviour is really made up of different criminal acts. During a riot there may be crimes against property, such as breaking windows, stealing goods from shops, and warehouses. It is quite common to see **looters,** laden with stolen clothes or electrical goods, disappearing from the scene of a riot. Cars and buses may be stolen and overturned, set on fire, or used as barricades against the police or army.

Fighting in a riot may lead to serious crimes of violence including personal injury and even rape or murder. Sometimes a group of enraged people takes the law into its own hands and executes someone on the street. A crowd which runs riot in any of these ways is usually called a **mob.** 'Mob rule' takes over when law and order breaks down.

In August 1991 tanks were brought on to the streets of Moscow in an attempt to stop political reforms. Protesters built barricades across the streets and threw petrol bombs at the tanks.

WHY DO RIOTS BREAK OUT?

Society is full of stresses and strains. Poverty, hunger or unemployment may make people desperate. Strikes and industrial disputes may burst into fighting or violence on the streets. Beliefs about politics, education or religion often arouse fierce passions. During times of uncertainty, the relationship between people of different ethnic backgrounds may become inflamed. People who speak a different language or follow a different way of life from the majority may be misunderstood or bullied by others.

Sometimes people riot in reaction to being treated with suspicion over a long period of time. When youths in one district of a city are constantly stopped and searched by police officers, their anger may turn to violent street protest against the authorities. Grudges may develop on both sides and the police may be accused of **harassment.** Prison officers too may face riotous behaviour, if the harsh conditions inside a jail cause a dangerous build-up of pressure.

Not all rioters are victims of poverty or oppression. Sports fans may riot after their team has lost. Rich youths may go on the rampage after celebrations at a night club or discotheque. Drunkenness has always been a common feature of riots. Weather conditions may also play a part. During hot weather, people gather out-of-doors in the streets. Here, rumours and local grievances can quickly blow up into violent behaviour.

UNRAVELLING THE PROBLEM

After a riot has taken place, an **official inquiry** may be set up to discover why it occurred. The answers are rarely simple or clear-cut. Many causes may overlap. A sincere political protest may be overtaken by looting and **vandalism.** During the breakdown of order, personal quarrels may flare up and old scores may be settled.

Official inquiries often result in more questions. How can riots be prevented? Do the police need to be more forceful, using more effective equipment to control the mob? Do we need to discover more about society and human behaviour? Can we solve the problem by declaring war on poverty and social injustice? These questions are often in the news, but neither they, nor the riots which often spark them off, belong just to the present.

ANGER THROUGH THE AGES

On 14 July 1789 a mob stormed the Bastille prison in Paris.
Men and women fought against the soldiers on guard. They
released prisoners and cut off the head of the prison
governor.

Writers may sometimes give the impression that history is made by individual rulers who seize or hold on to power. However, in 1743 the English politician Horace Walpole suggested that 'our supreme governors' were, in fact, 'the mob'. Certainly the angry reaction of the common people has often decided the course of history.

GREEKS AND ROMANS

Most ancient civilizations depended on slavery. Slaves were captured in war or bought and sold in the market place. They worked as labourers and servants and had few rights. Riots by slaves were common and sometimes turned into full-scale uprisings. In 464 BC the state of Sparta, in ancient Greece, was shaken by an earthquake. Law and order soon broke down. Rioting slaves took over the ruined streets and King Archidamus II was forced to lead his troops against the rebels in a series of pitched battles.

Ancient Greece also suffered from vandalism of the kind we know today. Reports from Athens in 415 BC told how drunken young aristocrats had smashed and defaced the many statues of the god Hermes, which stood at street corners in the city.

Throughout Rome's history, riots broke out over political disputes, over the shows in which gladiators fought to death in the arena, over slavery and over food supplies. In 121 BC the Roman government, or senate, voted to cancel laws which had been brought in to help the poor. Public riots broke out in the main square, or forum. Over 3000 people died in the disorder.

BLUES AGAINST GREENS

In AD 324 the Romans built a new eastern capital called Constantinople, on the site of the modern city of Istanbul. Constantinople became a hotbed of political intrigue, notorious for its rioting mob. In AD 532 the city burned for three days. When troops were brought in to attack rioters, 35 000 people were killed.

The riots were the result of fighting between political groups known as 'the 'Greens' and the 'Blues', who supported rival teams at the hippodrome, the stadium for chariot-racing. The emperor, Justinian, who was hated for bringing in harsh taxes, was accused of unfair support for the 'Blues'.

PRINCES AND PAUPERS

In western Europe the Middle Ages were marked by a series of violent uprisings, in which poor workers rioted against their rulers. In Paris in 1382 a woman trader attacked a tax collector and set off riots across the city. These were put down by troops. However, in restoring order the soldiers often ran riot themselves. They looted, raped and murdered in revenge.

The punishment for rioting was severe. In 1517 the streets of London were being made unsafe by gangs of youths. These apprentices were meant to be learning a trade, but they spent a lot of time in unruly behaviour. After a May Day riot in which they threw stones, broke windows and opened jails, thirteen of them were hanged by order of King Henry VIII. Others were paraded with nooses around their necks. The public blamed the king for over-reacting to the riot. It became known as 'Evil May Day'.

RELIGIOUS RIOTS

During the sixteenth and seventeenth centuries Protestant and Catholic Christians were bitterly divided. The differences often resulted in violence and cruelty on both sides. German Protestant troops occupied Rome in 1527. They ran riot, plundering, killing and burning for days. In 1545 Protestants in southern France were massacred, sold into slavery or burnt alive by Catholics. Churches, paintings and statues were destroyed during these troubled years.

RIOTS AND POLITICS

The London mob was never rowdier, or more powerful, than in the eighteenth century. Crowds were often violent and drunk with cheap gin. During elections, politicians paid them to riot, or to frighten off the opposition.

In the Gordon Riots of 1780, public feeling was whipped up by an anti-Catholic politician. Rioting broke out and over the next few days, several Roman Catholic chapels were destroyed. As the days of rioting wore on, the mob simply attacked the property of anyone who was wealthy. A valuable private library was destroyed and a distillery was broken open. Drunken rioters fell into the flames of burning buildings. Ten thousand troops were called in to restore order. The Gordon Riots shocked London's wealthier citizens, as they realized how their lives and property had so easily been put at risk.

READING THE RIOT ACT

During the seventeenth century, laws against rioting were introduced in Britain. Under the Riot Act of 1715, the local judge or magistrate had to publicly announce to the mob that normal laws were suspended, and that anyone who failed to leave the scene would be considered guilty. He could then use troops to restore order. Punishment was severe: rioters faced transportation to a prison colony overseas, or even death by hanging. The Riot Act remained in force for over two hundred years. It was last read in 1919.

'Our Sovereign Lord the King chargeth and commandeth all Persons, being assembled, immediately to disperse themselves, and peaceably to depart to their Habitations, or to their lawful Business, upon the Pains contained in the Act made in first year of King George, for preventing Tumults and riotous Assemblies. God Save the King!'

Proclamation of the Riot Act, Britain, 1715

A CRY FOR FREEDOM?

In the 1760s rioting over taxation broke out in Britain's American colonies, in New York and Boston. In 1772, colonists burnt British ships and covered tax collectors in tar and feathers. One year later, in 1773, American protesters against the British tax on tea boarded ships moored in Boston harbour, and tipped the cargo of tea into the water. This act was an important turning point in the worsening relations between Britain and the American colonies. It triggered off a whole set of even more unpopular laws, and by 1775 a full scale war of independence had started. The earlier riots had shown the strength of people's feelings, and they certainly played an important part in this period of change.

Sometimes, however, it is hard to return to peaceful government once the rule of law has broken down. During the French revolution of 1789, and the years immediately following it, many of those who had fought for freedom from poverty and unjust government lost control of the situation. The mob demanded more and more bloodshed. They were often led on by individual politicians eager to grab power for themselves. The years 1792–94 in particular were marked by uprisings, arrests and massacres, together known as 'the Terror'.

INDUSTRY AND REVOLUTION

The ideals of the French and American revolutions included freedom and equality for ordinary people. During the nineteenth century these ideals inspired people in other countries too. In England the working people of the growing industrial cities demanded political change, including the right to vote.

But at one large gathering on St Peter's Fields, Manchester, a crowd of 60 000 peaceful demonstrators was violently attacked by volunteer troops, mostly recruited from local businessmen. It was the troops that ran riot, not the demonstrators. They not only broke up the rally, but they killed two women, nine men and injured over 400 more. The year was 1819, four years after the famous battle of Waterloo, and the day became remembered as the 'Peterloo Massacre'.

By the end of the nineteenth century, there were many new political ideas gaining ground – about how a country should be run, and how its wealth should be shared. Some **anarchists** actually proposed riotous behaviour as a way of

Barcelona 1909: workers have barricaded the streets to stop the advance of government troops. The week of rioting was to result in widespread death and destruction.

resisting the oppressive laws of the state or the factory owners. In one 'tragic week' in 1909, Barcelona in Spain was the scene of widespread unrest. Shops and churches were looted, even graves were smashed. Trams were overturned, and many workers died fighting government troops. What had started as a general **strike** in the city ended in a reign of terror by the Spanish army.

'The argument of the broken pane of glass is the most valuable argument in modern politics.'

Emmeline Pankhurst, English campaigner for women's right to vote, 1912

'NIGHT OF GLASS'

Perhaps one of the most famous, and chilling riots in this century was recorded in **Nazi** Germany, just one year before the outbreak of the Second World War. Adolf Hitler and other Nazi leaders claimed to support law and order, but at the same time they carried out a systematic persecution of Jews in Germany.

During the night of 9 November 1938, in towns all over Germany, Nazi thugs smashed Jewish shops, businesses and homes, set synagogues on fire and beat up many innocent Jewish people, a number of whom died as a result. The rioters went unpunished, and the Jews were made to pay a fine of one billion marks for the damage, as well as repairing their own properties. *Kristallnacht* as it became known – on account of the broken glass that littered the pavements the next day – was a horrifying example of how a government can allow brutality to pass for lawful behaviour on its own streets.

Jewish shopkeepers sweep up broken glass after the *Kristallnacht* **riots in Berlin.**

COLONIAL UNREST

During the twentieth century the great empires that had grown up over the previous 200 years came to an end. Around the world, European powers such as France, Belgium, Portugal and Britain were forced to give independence to the overseas countries that they had once ruled as **colonies.** Demonstrations, and the riots which sometimes followed, were an important part of the struggle for freedom in many of the colonies. In 1942, 20 000 rioters took to the streets of Bombay. Their demand that the British should 'quit India' was repeated in many other Indian cities.

"BURN, BABY, BURN!"

Behind the scenes in the world's richest countries, there are still many people who live in very poor **ghettoes** and

Smoke darkens the sky above the streets of Los Angeles, California, as African American rioters set buildings on fire. The years 1965 – 8 were marked by severe riots in many American cities. 'Burn, baby, burn!' was a slogan of the day.

have little chance of improving their situation. In this century, as in earlier ones, their feelings of frustration and hopelessness have burst into violence, often spreading from one town to another.

During the 1960s, riots broke out in many cities across the United States. Many of the rioters were African Americans, weary of years of poverty, racial **discrimination** and ill-treatment. In 1965 the Watts area of Los Angeles was turned into a blazing inferno. An arrest for drunken driving sparked off the trouble. Looters raided stores. The bullets of **snipers** flew through the streets. Twenty-eight people were killed and over 600 were injured. Damage amounted to 175 million US dollars. The following years saw parts of Cleveland and New York ablaze. In 1968 the results of an inquiry into the riots by the Kerner Commission were published. They placed the blame firmly on white **racism,** unemployment, poor housing and police harassment.

> 'A riot is at bottom the language of the unheard.'
>
> *Martin Luther King, American civil*
> *rights campaigner, (1929-68)*

WHAT MAKES A RIOT?

In 1987 many South Koreans claimed that the results of an election had been fixed by the government. Thousands of people took to the streets. They threw petrol bombs at police and set fire to shops.

By looking at riots which have taken place in the past, we can see that they have common ingredients. Do certain conditions provide a breeding ground for riotous behaviour?

GOVERNMENT BREAKDOWN

The government of a country is responsible for maintaining order. When a government is weak it may be unable to do this. It may not have enough money to run the country's services properly. It may be unable to prevent corruption amongst its police officers.

In this kind of situation it is easy for protestors to believe that rioting will force the government to fall. Violence may be seen as the final push to bring a corrupt or inefficient system tumbling down. During 1990 rioters in many parts of the Soviet Union demanded political change. By the end of 1991 this country, the world's second most powerful nation, had broken up into separate independent states.

Rioting is usually disorganized and develops at a few moments' notice. It does not in itself change anything, and its results are sometimes uncertain. Rioters may lose public support if innocent people are injured. A riot may backfire, making conditions even worse than before. Lasting changes require careful organization, discussion and popular support.

> 'Thinkers prepare the revolution, bandits carry it out.'
>
> *Mariano Azuela, Mexican writer, 1918*

UNDER PRESSURE

If weak government encourages riotous behaviour, it might be argued that strong government and policing will prevent it. History tells us that this is not so. The stricter a government is, and the less **democratic,** the more likely it is to create a violent response. If peaceful protest is not allowed, or if people are harassed by police, the public may turn to violence. The repressive South Korean

SAINT BENEDICT SCHOOL
DUFFIELD ROAD
DERBY DE22 1JD

government faced repeated rioting during the 1980s, as vast crowds of opposition supporters demanded a political voice. Armed only with sticks, the protestors fought heavily armoured police on the streets of Seoul.

Perhaps the most rigidly controlled of all groups is found inside prison. The lives of convicts are controlled every minute of the day. They are locked away from society. And yet it is here that some of the most violent rioting breaks out – for the inmates believe that they have nothing left to lose. In September 1971 it took 1000 state troopers to storm New York's Attica state prison after four days of rioting by 1200 inmates. Putting down the riot cost 38 lives, including those of nine prison officers being held hostage.

Masked prisoners patrolling a cell block during the 1971 Attica riot. The riot was part of a desperate attempt to demand improved conditions.

A SENSE OF INJUSTICE

In 1984 Britain's coalminers were on strike. Their employers, the National Coal Board (NCB), intended to cut output, close 20 pits and get rid of 20 000 jobs in a year. The long, bitter dispute led to a great deal of violence. One of the worst clashes was at Orgreave, in South Yorkshire. Large numbers of riot police battled with striking miners. Many were injured. Police chiefs blamed the miners' leaders. However, the miners claimed that they were the victims of police violence which had been planned beforehand. They complained that the police were not neutral, but acting as political agents of the government and the NCB.

Many political decisions – from declaring war to changing the environment – may result in riots. In May 1978, Japanese anger over the site of Tokyo's new international airport boiled over into riots. The area looked like a battlefield as police with shields and truncheons struggled against ranks of demonstrators bearing banners and flags – and petrol bombs.

Sometimes a single event brings to the surface deep divisions and inequalities between people, and anger bursts into violence. In April 1992, a courtroom decision in Los Angeles sparked off widespread rioting, far worse than the Watts riots 27 years earlier. People from all over the world saw the video film that had been used as evidence in the case: it showed four Los Angeles police officers kicking and beating an African American while arresting him for a driving offence. The jury in the courtroom found all the policemen innocent of unlawful violence. As Los Angeles burned, people once again asked questions about the root causes of the violence.

'This is not an LA thing. We want the issue of racism addressed in all our communities. This is a national issue which needs a national programme.'

John Jacob, of the National Urban League in the United States, commenting on the 1992 riots

The anniversary of the Soweto rising was marked by new riots in 1980. Young people demanded social justice in South Africa. This girl was clubbed unconscious by riot police.

A BATTLE OF IDEAS

Schools and universities have been at the centre of trouble throughout history. It is here that young people debate new ideas and issues. It is here too that governments have always tried to impose the educational system that they approve of.

In June 1976 a major revolt broke out in Soweto, the poverty-stricken South African township, outside Johannesburg. Young blacks objected to a government ruling which forced them to learn Afrikaans in school. This language was associated with the racist laws of the white minority government. The police opened fire on the crowds without warning. Children threw stones at the police, protecting themselves with dustbin lids. There was **arson** and looting. One hundred people were killed and over 1000 were injured. Many were innocent children.

'Even initially, during the peaceful demonstrations, parents supported the pupils. But what really thrust the parents into action was the brutal police killings ... of young children ... Their hatred and rejection of the whole system came to the surface.'

Nkosazana Dlamini, campaigner against racism in South Africa, 1977

POVERTY AND HARDSHIP

Educational grievances may have been the flashpoint which set Soweto on fire in 1976. But there were other, deeper reasons. South African laws condemned all black citizens to a life of injustice, poverty and hardship in their own country. Around the world, most riots break out in poor areas, where people are deprived or hungry.

Some people have argued that rich countries should blame themselves for riots which break out in the poor parts of their towns and cities. They point out that in these countries, everyone is encouraged to 'consume' or buy goods. Advertisements on television and in glossy magazines tell everyone which goods they need if they are to be successful, attractive, or respected by others. Those who are trapped in unemployment and poverty may feel angry, frustrated, and forgotten. They have no hope of 'the good life' that is constantly being shown to them. Under certain conditions, this anger spills over into a riot, where symbols of wealth and success – such as cars and other expensive shop-window items – are destroyed.

CULTURE CLASH

Differences in ethnic background, way of life, language and religion make for a richly varied culture. Great civilizations take their strength from many sources. However, these differences may also lead to tension. Questions may arise such as the right of people to use their own language. Ignorance of other people's traditions may turn into racial or religious hatred. India for example is a

Police fire tear gas into the rioting crowd in Islamabad, Pakistan. This protest, in 1989, was against the publication of a book called *The Satanic Verses* by Salman Rushdie.

vast country which is home to a wide variety of peoples. In recent years it has seen severe rioting over both religion and language policies.

In 1988 a novel called *The Satanic Verses* was published in London. Many Muslims declared that the book was offensive to the Islamic faith. The Iranian leader, Ayatollah Khomeini, even issued a death sentence against the author, Salman Rushdie, who was forced to go into hiding. Riots broke out from Britain to Pakistan over the issue.

In 1991 riots against foreigners living in the eastern German town of Profen made many Europeans wonder if the ugly racial hatred of the Nazi period might return. Racial hatred was also being stirred up again in England and France. Had nothing been learned from history?

ON THE STREET, IN THE STADIUM

Youth riots sometimes seem to have no obvious cause other than drunkenness or boredom. On public holidays, for example, gangs of youths may go on the rampage. During the summers of the late 1960s, British seaside towns were shocked by a series of visits from rival city gangs known as 'Mods' and 'Rockers'. Fighting and rioting frequently broke out between these groups, as they 'took over' sea-front streets and parks. As the groups went out of fashion, these particular staged battles also came to an end.

Some of the most sudden and severe outbreaks of public violence in modern Europe have been at football matches. In 1985, soccer fans from Liverpool in England crowded into Belgium's Heysel stadium for a match against the Italian club, Juventus. Before the match started, rival supporters attacked each other with metal bars and flags. One charge of **hooligans** caused a wall to collapse. Forty-one fans were killed and over 350 injured.

THE MIND OF THE MOB

Looters run from a Los Angeles shoe shop during the 1992 riots. Whatever the cause of a riot, looting is a common follow-up, especially when people already feel angry and rebellious. Many, though, are quick to take advantage of the breakdown in law and order.

> 'Nor should we listen to those who say 'The voice of the people is the voice of God', for the turbulence of the mob is always close to insanity.'
>
> *Alcuin (AD 735-804),*
> *adviser to the Emperor Charlemagne*

Many acts of mob violence seem mindless. Even the most orderly and reasonable protests can be overtaken by violence. What makes people act in such a way?

Some people seem to take pleasure in destruction for the sake of it. They enjoy the sound of breaking glass. Riotous behaviour can be exciting. In times of danger the human body produces a chemical called adrenaline. This speeds up the heart and provides extra nervous energy.

Every day people put up with routine, with obeying orders, with behaving themselves. During a riot this normal world is overturned. People who normally have no power can get their own back, seek revenge, rule the streets for a day.

In ancient times many authorities actually encouraged rowdiness on certain days of the year. During a winter festival called Saturnalia the Romans were allowed to break certain laws without being punished, and the courts were closed. Slaves were waited upon by their masters. In the Middle Ages 'Lords of Misrule' were appointed at public festivals as a mockery of the forces of law and order. Such festivals seem to have served as safety valves – a way of allowing people to 'let off steam' without upsetting the order of life as a whole. Even today, carnival celebrations in many parts of the world have their roots in the same idea.

INDIVIDUALS AND GROUPS

When they are part of a large group, people often act as they never would on their own. They feel part of something else – something bigger than themselves. They may emphasize this by wearing similar clothes. Since the last century, youth gangs have chosen to identify themselves by their outrageous haircuts or their unusual fashions. These make them feel united with each other and at the same time different from everybody else. Football fans wear the colours of their team. These too encourage the idea of belonging to a group. Soldiers are issued with uniforms for the same reason.

Once they are part of a group, people tend to feel less responsible for their own actions. An individual's personal sense of right or wrong is often lost or overruled. Some may be afraid to stop any violence that breaks out, in case other members of the group think they are cowards. Others may try to show off, aiming to shock or out-perform other group members.

Some of the worst examples of such behaviour have occurred when troops run riot during a war. In 1968, during the Vietnam War, US troops ran out of control while patrolling a village called My Lai. They murdered innocent women and children, killing 567. Such people would not have been murderers at home. They had become brutalized by fear and warfare. The same kind of personality change can occur during riots on city streets.

> '"Hush," replied Mr Pickwick. "...It's always best on these occasions to do what the mob do."
> "But supposing there are two mobs?" suggested Mr Snodgrass.
> "Shout with the largest," replied Mr Pickwick.'
>
> *From 'Pickwick Papers,' by Charles Dickens, 1836*

Young men are often in the front line of a riot. However, women too have taken part in riots throughout history. They were very active in the mob during the French revolution, when they were often feared more than the men. Briefly, they enjoyed an equality that they had not known before, in the home. On the streets they were all 'citizens'. The suffragettes, who campaigned for women's votes in the early twentieth century, were prepared to smash windows and create wide-scale disorder. Young women also played a prominent part in the London 'poll tax' riot of 1990.

RABBLE ROUSERS

Crowds are emotional. Football crowds chant and shout. Political rioters may sing revolutionary songs or chant slogans. Marches may be led by drummers or musicians playing rousing anthems or marching tunes. Even the rhythmic banging of dustbin lids may put fear into the 'enemy'. During the industrial conflicts of the 1980s, British riot police beat their shields rhythmically with their truncheons in an attempt to scare the crowds.

Most successful politicians know how to play with the emotions of a crowd. Wise speakers will try to use the calm voice of reason. However, others may use their skill to stir

Supporters of the AWB, an extreme 'white power' group in South Africa, join hands with their leader Eugene Terreblanche and wave Nazi-style flags as they break up a political meeting in 1986.

up a frenzy of strong feeling. Within a rioting mob there may be a ringleader or an **agitator,** urging people on in this way.

Not all agitators are what they seem. It is common for the police or the government to place their own agents in a crowd in order to make trouble. These are known by a French term, **agents provocateurs.** They may act as spies or as informers. They may be there to ensure that peaceful demonstrators are discredited and made to look like criminals.

IMAGES OF VIOLENCE
The religious riots of the sixteenth and seventeenth centuries followed the invention of printing. Pamphlets were passed from hand to hand, encouraging people to rise up and attack their opponents. Today, popular newspapers may use words which encourage racist or political thuggery.

Television holds even more power over people's minds. Some people blame the images of violence shown in films for an increasingly lawless society. It has been suggested that the presence of television cameras encourages people to act up and show off, turning a demonstration into a riot. It certainly brings home to people the fact that they are making news, and gives them a sense of their own importance.

Television news reporting clearly has an effect on public disorder. People who see that rioting is taking place in one city may do the same elsewhere. This 'copycat' violence may have contributed to some of the British city riots in 1981 and 1991. It is unlikely that the governments of eastern Europe would have fallen so quickly in recent years, if television and radio broadcasts had not shown people the unrest that was taking place in neighbouring countries.

THE ANGER PASSES
A popular rising or a revolution unfolds over a period of time. However, a riot normally lasts a short while, a few hours or a single night. Then, often suddenly, the anger is

SAINT BENEDICT SCHOOL
DUFFIELD ROAD
DERBY DE22 1JD

spent. People sober up. The effects of alcohol wear off. Those who have not been arrested go home or drift away.

Next day, looking at the damage they have caused, they may themselves feel surprised at the action they took. For they are no longer part of a crowd, but individuals once more.

> 'For violent fires soon burn out themselves...'
>
> *From 'Richard II,' by William Shakespeare, 1595*

LAW AND ORDER

Italian police fire tear gas into the crowd as rioting breaks out
at an England – Belgium football match in Turin in 1980.

Riots normally occur suddenly and unexpectedly. This means that the **security forces** must be ready for action anywhere, at any time. They must be especially prepared during large demonstrations, celebrations or sporting events which are likely to turn violent.

POLICING CROWDS

Decisions must be made. Which of the security forces should be used? In many countries there are special squads for dealing with crowd control. In the United States, the National Guard, a volunteer local militia, may be brought in for serious riots. During the riots at Newark, New Jersey, in 1967, US President Johnson made history by bringing in federal paratroopers.

Discussions are normally held with the organizers of demonstrations or sporting events weeks beforehand, in order to prevent trouble breaking out. The police may ask the demonstrators to provide their own stewards to keep order. They agree a route which is acceptable. Rival marchers or sports fans must where possible be kept apart, to avoid fighting breaking out.

On the day, helicopters may be used to monitor the progress of the crowds. Security vehicles may bear large numbers on the roof for easy identification from the air. Police officers on the ground may be in radio contact with the control room, which is often based in a mobile van. Police reserves may be bussed in to the area, but kept out of sight. Police horses and leashed dogs, specially trained to control crowds, keep people in line.

WHEN RIOTING STARTS

If fighting does break out, the police horses may charge the crowd while riot squads advance down the street. High-powered hoses called water cannon may be used to knock people to the ground. In Amsterdam, in the Netherlands, they have in the past been fitted to boats on the city's many canals. They are more normally fixed to armoured vehicles, which can also fire **tear gas** or perhaps lay down barbed-wire barricades. If a full-scale rising looks likely, tanks may be sent out on the streets.

'Snatch' squads may be sent into a rioting crowd by the security forces. Their aim is to seize trouble makers and carry them away to be arrested. In the confusion, it is common for innocent people to be carried off. The police may use video cameras to identify individuals in the crowd.

FROM DEFENCE TO ATTACK

Special clothing for individual police officers or soldiers is designed to protect the wearer from attack by the crowd, who may be carrying weapons such as axes, knives, spears, clubs or firearms. Riot gear usually includes boots, a shield, and a specially designed helmet which protects the face and neck. A bullet-proof vest or jacket provides protection against sniper fire. Personal weapons may include truncheons, long sticks (known in India as *lathis*), whips (the South African *sjambok*), or firearms.

Firearms may be designed to fire plastic bullets. These are meant only to stun, but they can in practice kill people. Sometimes live shots are fired above the crowd as a warning. This may be effective in scattering a crowd, but it also increases the risk of death and injury. On one particular Sunday in the city of Londonderry, Northern Ireland, British soldiers fired into a crowd of demonstrators who were protesting against imprisonment without trial in the province. They killed fourteen unarmed civilians. The army claimed that shots had first been fired at them by hidden snipers, but the day – 30 January 1972 – is still remembered as 'Bloody Sunday'.

HOW MUCH FORCE?

A violent riot places the security forces in a difficult position. If they fail to send in a large number of officers, they may be unable to control part of the city. A no-go area like this allows the rioters to claim victory and to break the law freely.

However, just as much trouble can be caused if the authorities are panicked into over-reacting to a very large demonstration. The sudden appearance of heavily armed riot police may anger or frighten the crowd and so make the trouble worse. If someone is injured or killed by the riot squad, the crowd may react with fury. News pictures of such events may show the police beating individuals and so make nonsense of the idea that the police are there to keep the peace.

> 'Policemen should ... shoot arsonists to kill and looters to maim. You wouldn't want to shoot children, but with Mace (teargas) you can detain youngsters.'
>
> *Briefing for police officers by Richard Daley, Mayor of Chicago, 1968*

CLEARING THE STREETS

In recent years some British politicians have called for the Riot Act to be re-introduced, so that the streets can be rapidly cleared of rioters. They have ignored the fact that this law was never effective, even when it was in force. Mobs move quickly and do not wait around to hear an official announcement that they have become criminals by being there. The most likely people to fall foul of a Riot Act are confused passers-by.

Special laws are often passed if a series of riots persists over a long period. A state of emergency may be declared, or even martial law. The latter gives the armed forces sweeping powers of arrest and detention. A curfew may be announced, which requires people to stay at home overnight, or between certain hours.

QUESTIONS OF LAW

In some countries, arrested rioters may be beaten up. They may then face illegal torture, imprisonment without trial or even death. In countries which recognize the rule of law, penalties may still be severe. In most countries rioters may expect to pay a large fine or go to jail.

In the United States and Britain, most riot trials revolve around questions of a 'breach of the peace' – in other words, illegal fighting in a public place.

In France however, the term 'riot' is included under the

Who is keeping the peace and who is breaking it? At this 1987 protest in Pakistan a striker is being beaten and kicked by a policeman.

more serious charge of 'rebellion'. In some countries the term 'riot' refers only to clashes with the security forces.

LONG-TERM SOLUTIONS
The gallows and dungeons of the Middle Ages did not stop people rioting. From 1919 to 1933 the United States banned the sale of alcohol. This did not prevent riotous behaviour. Indeed, it encouraged gang warfare as criminals moved in to control the trade. In recent years, the increased use of riot gear, modern communications and weapons by the security forces have also failed to prevent rioting.

After Britain's 1981 inner city riots, an official report by Lord Scarman suggested that longer-term measures were needed. The root problems of poverty, inequality and injustice, needed to be tackled. Education should be in the forefront of the drive against lawlessness, religious and racial hatred. Police officers should be known personally within the communities where they operate.

The small details of change must not be forgotten either. For example, it seems more likely that disorder occurs in traditional soccer stadiums where spectators are herded onto open terraces or placed behind 'cages'. European clubs are now learning lessons from American football stadiums. These are designed for family comfort and everyone has a seat.

RIGHT OR WRONG ?

A crowd of young people confronts armed British troops in Northern Ireland. Disorder on the streets raises important questions, for protesters and for the forces of law and order.

People's opinions about riots often differ. After a series of disturbances in British towns in 1991, the Archbishop of Canterbury blamed social problems for the trouble. He pointed out that the riots had occurred on run-down housing estates, in areas of high unemployment. However, a priest working in one of these areas claimed that the riots were the work of young hooligans who did not know, or care about, the difference between right and wrong. Individuals were themselves to blame, not the conditions in which they lived.

Most people would agree that individuals have a responsibility to themselves and others; rioting is irresponsible because it can destroy people's lives and possessions. It is reasonable to expect parents and teachers to educate children so that they do not behave in this way.

However, governments have a responsibility, too. Their duty to the individual is to provide justice, freedom of expression, to create opportunities for people to improve their lives, and to fight poverty and discrimination. Many of the examples in this book have shown that rioting is very often a last resort for people who have lost hope of ever achieving these things.

PEACEFUL PROTEST

Do those who wish to change society have any other alternatives? Is there a more moral form of protest? During the campaign for independence in India, the great Indian leader Mohandâs Gandhi insisted that all protest should be non-violent. India became independent in 1947. How successful were Gandhi's methods? He was in fact unable to prevent rioting taking place. When parts of India were made into the separate Muslim state of Pakistan, rioting between Hindu and Muslim mobs broke out on a terrible scale. Gandhi grieved as thousands were massacred. Nevertheless, Gandhi's moral example came to be admired all over the world. He had shown that alternatives to violent protest do exist.

It often requires great bravery for an individual to resist group pressure and act according to his or her conscience. Germans who protested about Nazi brutality in the 1930s

A 1983 rally in Washington DC demands 'peace, jobs and freedom'. Twenty years earlier the great African American leader Martin Luther King had spoken here about his dream of changing society by peaceful methods. He was murdered in 1968.

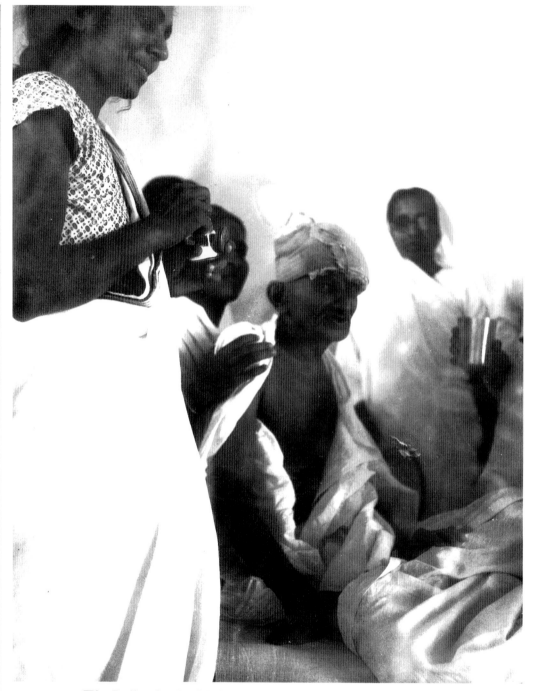

The Indian leader Mohandâs Gandhi refused to eat, as a
form of non-violent political protest. However, many of his
supporters did resort to rioting.

disappeared from the streets and were never seen again. Non-violent protest may not be effective in a police state.

MORAL MAZES

Most religions condemn riotous behaviour. However, religions have themselves been a major reason for rioting throughout history. Many political groups claim to seek social justice, and yet use violence as a way of gaining power and influence. Governments which talk the most about law and order are often those which allow their security forces to terrorize the public.

Of course this does not mean that all religious or political leaders are hypocritical. It simply means that it is hard to live up to ideals. Human nature makes it very difficult to turn political or religious dreams into reality.

For the victims of riot, the moral rights and wrongs may be overshadowed by their own sense of loss afterwards. Whatever the cause of a riot, the result nearly always includes destruction of property, personal injury, or, in extreme cases, death. Those who suffer most may be those least able to defend or help themselves — such as the elderly lady who lost her own small home above a burnt out shop in the 1992 Los Angeles riots.

People often argue about who is in the right in a riot situation. Soldiers who run riot may plead that they are only obeying orders. A group of rioters may kill a captive because they believe him or her to be a government spy, working for their downfall. Members of the Romanian secret police, the *securitate*, were lynched by rioters after the fall of Nicolae Ceaucescu's oppressive government in Romania.

The problem of public disorder is unlikely to disappear in the twenty-first century. As long as starvation exists,

---

The limitation of riots, moral questions aside, is that they cannot win, and their participants know it.

Martin Luther King, American civil rights campaigner, (1929-68)

people will riot. As long as people suffer unjust government, they will riot. As long as people are brought up in ignorance or prejudice, they may act as bullies towards other peoples and cultures. It is sometimes not enough for individuals to stand up alone for what is right. They must join together on an international basis and work for peace.

'Rebellion to tyrants is obedience to God.'

Epitaph of John Bradshaw (1602-59), who sentenced King Charles I of England to death. Later, the motto of Thomas Jefferson, US President (1743-1826)

KEY DATES

BC 464
Slave revolt Slaves seize chance to riot after earthquake in Sparta.

BC 415
Vandalism in ancient Greece Drunken youths smash religious statues in Athens.

AD 532
'Blues against Greens' Political agitators and sports hooligans set Constantinople ablaze.

1381
Peasants against taxes The Peasants' Revolt in England grows from a protest into a riot. Though their leader is killed, the King pardons most of the protesters and the tax is dropped.

1500s and 1600s
Catholics and Protestants Christianity at war with itself. Widespread riots, massacres, disorder.

1715
Clearing the streets by law Britain brings in the Riot Act, to be read out to offenders.

1772
The rough road to liberty Riots against unfair taxes lead to American war of independence.

1819
Troops run riot Volunteer forces, representing local businessmen, break up a peaceful workers' rally in England, killing and injuring many in the 'Peterloo Massacre'.

1909
City on fire Widespread riots spill over from workers' strike in Barcelona, Spain.

1938
Government-sponsored race riot Racist thugs in Germany smash Jewish shops and synagogues and beat Jews with the blessing of the Nazis.

1942
End of empire Riots indicate tension in 'quit India' campaign.

1965
Cry from the ghetto Riots in poor parts of many cities in the United States.

1976
Front-line children In Soweto, South Africa, schoolchildren protest against learning Afrikaans. Riots follow, and many are killed or injured by police.

1985
A game of violence? Rival fans riot at an international football match in Belgium, with fatal results.

1989
The power of the pen Riots in Pakistan against the publication of *The Satanic Verses* by Salman Rushdie.

1991
Overthrowing the old order The people of Moscow riot against army tanks on the city's streets, showing their refusal to return to life under the old political system.

GLOSSARY

agent provocateur A police or government secret agent who joins rioters or conspirators in order to encourage them to commit illegal acts.

agitator Somebody who stirs up trouble in a crowd.

anarchist Someone who believes that people should organize themselves by loose agreements between individuals and groups rather than by a powerful government. While some anarchists believe in non-violence, others argue that state government should be over thrown by any means necessary.

arson The illegal burning down of a building.

colony Land or territory governed by a more powerful country.

democratic Allowing government by the people, with voting rights for all adult citizens.

discrimination Unfair treatment of one section of the community.

ethnic minority A group of people who share a language or cultural background that is different from that of most of the population.

ghetto An area of a city in which an ethnic minority is forced to live. During the Middle Ages, ghettoes for Jews were set up in European cities such as Venice. Today the term is also used to describe any poor or depressed part of a city.

harassment The persistent tormenting or troubling of an individual or a group. Police harassment of youths on the street may trigger off a riot. Police officers themselves may be harassed by youth gangs.

hooligan Someone who engages in mindless disorder or vandalism. The name is said to have come from 'Hooley's gang' a nineteenth century London street gang.

looter Someone who takes advantage of public disorder in order to break into buildings such as shops, homes or warehouses and steal the contents.

mob An angry crowd engaged in riot or illegal violence.

Nazi A short name for the German National Socialist Workers' Party which seized power in 1933 under Adolf Hitler and promoted racist ideas. It allowed no opposition to its views.

official inquiry (into a riot) A commission set up by the government to consider the reasons for the riot, the way in which it was policed etc.

racism The belief that one type of human being is essentially different from or superior to another.

riot A violent and undisciplined disturbance created by a group of people.

security forces Organizations with the power to keep public order, such as the army or the police.

sniper Somebody who shoots at individuals from a hidden position.

strike Refusing to continue work until particular demands are agreed.

tear gas A gas used in riot control, which makes the eyes water and ache, and can cause breathing difficulties.

vandalism Mindless destruction or damage of buildings, amenities, works of art etc. The word comes from the Vandals, a Germanic people whose soldiers sacked Rome in AD 455.

SAINT BENEDICT SCHOOL
DUFFIELD ROAD
DERBY DE22 1JD

INDEX